Word Mastery Series

Reading and Language Arts

NEW LEAF

New Leaf Education
P. O. Box 16230
Baltimore, Maryland 21211

New Leaf Education has a special offer on new products
for people on our mailing list.
Go to www.newleafeducation.com to learn more.

Design and Cover Illustration:
Ophelia M. Chambliss
Oliver Bliss Design

Printed in the United States of America

10 9 8 7 6 5 4 3 2 1

NEW LEAF

Contents

Essential Words

welcome to the

Essential Words

Reading and Language Arts
GLOSSARY!

ABOUT THE BOOK

Here is a glossary to help you learn the Essential Words you will need to be successful in school. These Essential Words will also help you succeed on state tests. There are almost 200 Reading and Language Arts words in the book! They are listed in alphabetical order under six main topics.

Here is a sample word with its features:

Picture to help understanding   **Easy-to-read definitions**

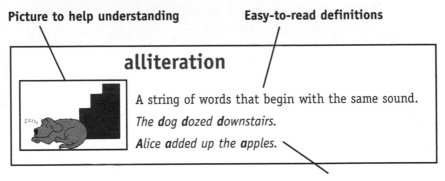

alliteration

A string of words that begin with the same sound.

*The **d**og **d**ozed **d**ownstairs.*

***A**lice **a**dded up the **a**pples.*

Example in context

We hope that you will find this book easy to use and enjoyable. Tell us what you think. We would love to hear from you!
www.newleafeducation.com

WORD RECOGNITION

antonym

A word that has the opposite meaning of another word.

*The antonym of **cold** is **hot**.*

connotative meaning

The secondary, or suggested, meaning of a word.

*The connotative meaning of **snake** is something that is evil, sneaky, or dangerous.*

consonants

Letters in the alphabet that can join with a **vowel** to make a **syllable**; when consonants are spoken, the breath is at least partly blocked.

The consonants in the English alphabet are

b, c, d, f, g, h, j, k, l, m, n, p, q, r, s, t, v, w, x, z, and sometimes y.

context clues

The parts of a sentence that are near a word and help to explain its meaning.

*The boats were tied tightly to poles at the end of the **dock**.*

In this sentence, the context clues "tie tightly to poles" tell the reader that a dock is a place to tie up or park boats.

WORD RECOGNITION

denotative meaning

The primary, or main, meaning of a word.

*The literal, or denotative, meaning of **snake** is "a long, scaly reptile with no limbs."*

homophone

A word that sounds like another word but has a different meaning or spelling.

***To, two,** and **too** all sound alike but have different spellings and different meanings.*

idiom

A saying that means something different from what it seems to say.

It's raining cats and dogs.
Let's call it a day.

multiple meaning word

A word that has more than one meaning or definition.

*We are having **company** for dinner.*
*My father got a job at a new **company***

WORD RECOGNITION

origin

Where a word comes from.

The word market *comes from the Latin word* mercari, *meaning "to trade."*

prefix

A letter or group of letters added to the beginning of a word to change its meaning.

In the words **unfair, dislike,** *and* **midterm,** *the prefixes are* **un-, dis-,** *and* **mid-.**

Examples of prefixes and their meanings:

dis-	do the opposite of	**dis**appear
il-	not	**il**legal
mis-	badly	**mis**behave
re-	again	**re**write
un-	not	**un**skilled

root

The most basic part of a word, to which prefixes and suffixes are added.

The root of the word **reaction** *is* **act.**

WORD RECOGNITION

suffix

A letter or group of letters added to the end of a word to change its meaning.

*In the words **kingdom**, **vacation**, and **smiling**, the suffixes are* **-dom, -tion,** *and* **-ing**.

Examples of suffixes:

Noun suffixes	-ness	dark**ness**
	-er	play**er**
	-or	act**or**
	-ship	friend**ship**
Adjective suffixes	-able	enjoy**able**
	-ful	beauti**ful**
	-ous	graci**ous**
	-less	pain**less**
Verb suffixes	-en	light**en**
	-ify	beaut**ify**
	-ize	special**ize**
Adverb suffix	-ly	quick**ly**

syllable

A unit of sound in a word.

*The word **cat** has one syllable.*
*The word **basket** has two syllables. (bas-ket)*
*The word **bicycle** has three syllables. (bi-cy-cle)*

WORD RECOGNITION

synonym

A word that means the same or about the same as another word.

A synonym for **large** *is* **big**.

vowels

Letters in the alphabet that can make a **syllable** on their own; when vowels are spoken, the breath is not blocked.

The vowels in the English alphabet are **a, e, i, o, u,** *and sometimes* **y.**

analyze

To study the relationship between different people, events, or things.

In The Adventures of Tom Sawyer, *you can analyze why Tom likes pretending to be a robber.*

caption

caption

A description of the people, places, or things shown in a picture. It is usually found near the picture.

The caption under the picture tells that the firefighter saved the cat.

cause

The reason an event or an **effect** happens.

Because of the rainstorm, Javier bought an umbrella.

The rainstorm was the cause of Javier's buying the umbrella.

cause-and-effect chart

A diagram that shows how **causes** and **effects** are connected.

In the cause-and-effect chart, we listed Hurricane Bob as the cause, and the loss of electricity and fallen trees as the effects.

Cause:	Effect:	Effect:
Hurricane Bob	loss of electricty	fallen trees

compare

To show how people, places, or things are similar or the same.

When you compare two characters in a story, you might describe how both have the same clothes, or how they enjoy doing the same things.

contrast

To show how people, places, or things are different.

When you contrast two characters in a story, you might describe how they have different hair color, or how one is friendly and one is not.

details

Sentences in a passage or paragraph that tell about the **main idea**.

Mexico is a great place. **The food is delicious. Fiestas are fun. The people are friendly and helpful.**

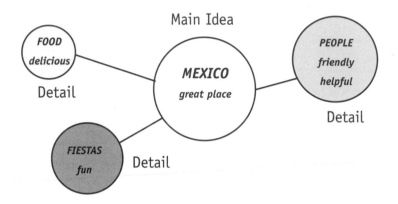

draw conclusions

To use information given in a passage to understand what the author is saying or what the story is about.

Anne Frank hid with her family for years in a friend's attic. They were often afraid to make even a sound. Their friends told no one they were there. **It was a dangerous time.**

effect

The result of an event or a **cause**.

Because of the rainstorm, Javier bought an umbrella.

Javier's buying an umbrella was an effect of the rainstorm.

READING STRATEGIES

essential information

The most important **facts** and **details** to know.

The essential information in a passage about caring for a pet goldfish could include, "Feed 5 or 6 flakes of food every three days."

evaluate

To study and understand the value of something.

You can evaluate what makes a story funny or sad, or why a character is a hero for solving a problem.

fact

A true statement, something that can be proven.

Water turns to ice when it freezes.
This is a fact that can be shown to be true.

generalization

A statement that describes a whole group of people or things based on facts about a few people or things.

*To say "Everybody likes rice" is a **generalization**, because not every person in the world likes rice. Generalizations may not be true in all cases.*

Reading Strategies

graphic organizer

A diagram used to show information to help the reader understand a passage.

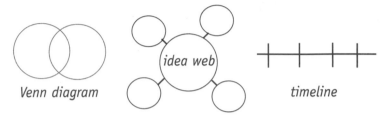

Venn diagram   idea web   timeline

heading

A title that tells what a section in a passage is about.

In a passage about sports, all of the sentences under the heading "Water Sports" should be about only those sports that are played in the water.

idea web

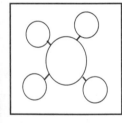

A **graphic organizer** that arranges the **main idea** of a passage and all of the **details** that support it.

key words

The most important terms in a passage that you need to learn and remember.

*The Amazon River is the **second longest** river in the world. It is about **4,000 miles (6,436 km) long**. It has the most water of any river in the world. Ships can sail as far as **2,300 miles (3,701 km)** up the Amazon.*

ReADiNg stRAtegieS

main idea

What a passage or paragraph is about.

*All modern cars are fitted with seat belts. Tires do not blow out so easily. Strong frames and air bags help protect passengers in an accident. **In many ways, cars today are safer than ever.***

make inferences

To use information that you already know to guess about something that is not directly said in a passage.

You may be told in a story that one character doesn't smile or have any friends. From this, and from what you know about people, you make the inference that the character is unhappy.

nonessential information

The less important **details** and **facts** in a passage.

The nonessential information in a passage about caring for a pet goldfish could include: "You can add colorful rocks or figures of divers to make your aquarium more interesting."

opinion

A statement of what someone thinks about something.

Carlie thought the movie was terrible, but Maria thought it was great.

REAdiNg stRAtegies

paraphrase

To rewrite a passage in your own words.

When you write a summary of a passage, you paraphrase the author's words and sentences, but still tell the same idea.

Original: These are the times that try men's souls.
Paraphrase: These are hard times for everyone.

predict

To think about or guess what might happen next in a passage.

Diego could predict what would happen at the end of the story because he looked for clues while he was reading.

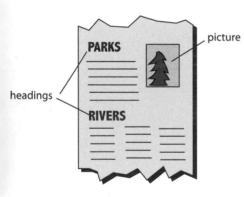

preview

To look over a passage before reading it to understand what it is about.

You can preview a passage by reading the headings, looking at the pictures, and reading the passage quickly to get an idea of what it is about.

problem

Something that needs to be solved.

In a story about a missing dog, the problem is how to find the lost dog.

record

To write down information as you read.

If you record your ideas while you're reading a passage, they can help you remember the most important parts of the passage.

sequence

The order in which events happen or in the way the author tells a story.

First, Marco went to the grocery store. Then, he stopped at the library. Finally, he took the bus home. That is the sequence of events in Marco's morning.

1, 2, 3

solution

An answer, or the way to fix a **problem**.

The solution in a story about a missing dog is how someone finds the dog.

summarize

To retell the most important things that happen in a passage.

A Night to Remember tells the true story of the great ocean liner Titanic. The ship was supposed to be unsinkable. But on its very first trip, it hit an iceberg and sank.

timeline

A **graphic organizer** that shows when, or on what dates, certain events took place.

Hamid used a timeline to show important events in his life. He noted when he was born, when he started school, and when he joined the baseball team.

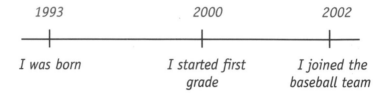

1993	2000	2002
I was born	I started first grade	I joined the baseball team

time order

The sequence of events shown in the order of what happened first to what happened last.

This story is in time order:

When Etsu was getting ready to go to school one morning, she couldn't find her Language Arts homework. She looked everywhere. Then the school bus came and she had to leave. All morning she worried about her homework. That afternoon, in her Language Arts class, her teacher said, "Look, Etsu. Here's your homework. Your mother found it and brought it to school." When Etsu went home, she was happy.

Clue words showing time order in the story: When, Then, All morning, That afternoon, When.

ReADiNg stRAtegies

Venn diagram

A **graphic organizer** that uses overlapping circles to show the relationship between two things or ideas and how they are alike and different.

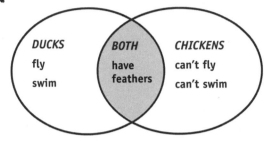

act (of a play or drama)

One of the major parts of a play, often divided into **scenes**.

In Act I of the play, we get to know the characters and the conflict

alliteration

A string of words that begin with the same sound.

*The **d**og **d**ozed **d**ownstairs.*
***A**lice **a**dded up the **a**pples.*

allusion

A reference to a real or fictional person, event, or place.

The teacher made an allusion to the watch carried by the White Rabbit in Alice in Wonderland.

autobiography

A **narrative** in which someone tells about his or her own life.

When I write my autobiography, I will talk about growing up on a farm.

Literary Concepts

biography

A **narrative** that tells about another person's life.

The new biography of George Washington tells how he defeated the English.

cast

The actors who play the roles in a play or movie.

The cast of Peter Pan *included several sixth graders.*

characterization

The way an author describes the looks, actions, and thoughts of a character, and how others think about that character.

In the book To Kill a Mockingbird, *Atticus Finch is a good man of strong morals. As a father, he tries to raise his two children to treat others fairly. The people in his town turn to him for advice and help.*

conflict

The clash between persons or forces that leads to the action in a story.

In the movie, the conflict was between two families who wanted to own the same land.

Literary Concepts

dialogue

The talking between two or more characters in a play.

> "Hi, Roberto. How are you?" said Andy.
>
> "Great. And you?" asked Roberto.
>
> "Just fine," said Andy.
>
> "Good," said Roberto.

drama (or play)

A story that is written to be performed by actors in a theater.

William Shakespeare wrote 38 dramas. One of them was Romeo and Juliet.

fable

A **narrative** that teaches a lesson using animal characters.

All summer long the grasshopper was making music, while the ant was working hard to have food during the winter.

Once the cold set in, the ant could rest in her warm home and enjoy three meals a day. The grasshopper was freezing and starving. The ant had a good heart and asked the grasshopper to spend the winter with her. She said: "All summer long your fine music made my life easier, now I'm making yours easier."

Literary Concepts

fiction

A **narrative** made up from a writer's imagination.
Novels and *short stories* are works of fiction.

Once upon a time, there was a poor girl named Cinderella. With her fairy godmother's help, she met the prince. They fell in love and lived happily ever after.

figurative language

Expressions used to create a special effect or feeling.

Zoe felt on top of the world when she won first prize.

This means she felt very happy.

flashback

A jump backward in time to an earlier part of a story.

When Maria saw the picture of her on her tenth birthday, she suddenly felt she was at her party that day.

foreshadow

To use hints or clues to suggest what will happen later in a **narrative**.

In the movie, the sudden storm foreshadows the flood that happens near the end.

genre

A type or kind of literature.

*The three major genres of literature are **poetry, drama**, and the **novel**.*

historical fiction

A fictional narrative set in a specific period in history.

The book A Bold Journey West with Lewis and Clark *is an example of historical fiction.*

hyperbole

An exaggeration used to draw attention to something.

"I told you a million times to get out of bed," my mother said to me.

legend

A story of a hero from the past, either real or fictional.

The stories about King Arthur and the knights of the Round Table are legends.

metaphor

A figure of speech that compares one thing to another without using the words *like* or *as*.

He had a **heart of stone**.

meter

The pattern of stresses in words, used to create rhythm in a poem.

The **mer**ry bells **ring**
To **wel**come the **Spring**.

mood

The feeling given to the reader by a piece of writing.

The mood in this paragraph is scary.

It was dark outside. Jenny sat by her lamp and read a book. She could hear a door creak slowly open downstairs. Then she heard slow, heavy steps on the stairs. Jenny's heart began to beat faster and faster.

myth

A traditional story that tries to explain natural events, usually with superhuman beings or gods.

In Greek myth, the gods forced Atlas to carry the world on his shoulders.

narrative

A story.

Once upon a time, a king lived with his queen. They worked hard and had many adventures together. When their son was old enough to be king, they retired. From then on, they lived happily ever after.

nonfiction

A piece of writing that is based on facts.

In his nonfiction book Travels with Charlie, *John Steinbeck tells about his drive around the United States with his dog Charlie.*

novel

A long story, usually with a complicated **plot** and many characters.

Margaret Mitchell wrote only one novel – Gone with the Wind.

personification

A figure of speech that speaks of a thing as if it were a person.

It was a bright day, and the sun smiled down on us.

Literary Concepts

playwright

The author of a play or **drama**.

Lope de Vega, the Spanish playwright who lived at the same time as Shakespeare, wrote more than 1,800 plays.

plot

The string of connected events in a story.

The Wizard of Oz *is about a girl named Dorothy, whose house drops down into a magical land after a tornado. She has many adventures before she finds a way to return to her beloved home in Kansas.*

poetry

Writing that usually has a rhythm, uses figures of speech, sometimes rhymes, and is usually arranged in lines.

I found a sea shell near my feet
As I kick the sand
I pick it up and look to see
How small it is in my hand
And as the ocean calls my name
I know what I must do
Return my shell just the same
To that water deep and blue

point of view

The telling of events in a story as one of the characters sees them.

First person point of view ("I"): As soon as I saw him, I could see that it was my old friend from school. I jumped to my feet and hugged him. I felt happy inside.
Third person point of view ("he," "she," or "they"): Sandro looked at the mountain. He knew it would be hard to climb. But he had to try.

LiterARy ConCeptS

resolution

The ending of a story when the main **conflict** has been solved.

In The Call of the Wild, *the resolution happens when Buck returns to the wild after losing his human friend, John Thornton.*

scene

A part of an **act** in a **play**.

In the first scene of the play Macbeth, *the witches plan to meet with the main character.*

setting

The time and place in which a play or story takes place.

The setting of John Steinbeck's book The Pearl *is La Paz, Mexico, in the 1940s.*

short story

A brief fictional **narrative**, usually with a simple **plot** and few characters.

"The Tell-Tale Heart" is a short story by Edgar Allan Poe. It tells how a man's guilt for his crime against someone else finally drives him mad.

Literary Concepts

simile

A figure of speech that compares two unlike things using the words *like* or *as*.

*Her hair is **like silk**.*

stage

A space in which actors perform a play.

The first actor to come on stage was someone playing a juggler.

stanza

A group of lines in a poem.

These are two stanzas from a poem:

> In winter, when the fields are white,
> I sing this song for your delight.
> In spring, when woods are getting green,
> I'll try and tell you what I mean.
>
> In summer, when the days are long,
> Perhaps you'll understand the song.
> In autumn, when the leaves are brown,
> Take a pen and ink, and write it down.

style

An author's particular way of writing.

Ernest Hemingway's writing style is clear and to the point.

ℒⁱteRARy coNCeptſ

symbol

An object used to represent an idea or meaning.

The rose is a common symbol of beauty.

tall tale

A story that couldn't happen in real life.

Paul Bunyan was a lumberjack of great size and strength. He is a hero of tall tales. Paul and his blue ox Babe were so large that their footsteps created Minnesota's ten thousand lakes.

theater

A building or room for presentating live plays or movies.

Plays are usually performed in a theater, but some are performed in the open air.

Most movie theaters can show many films at once.

theme

The message or point of a story. A story might have several themes.

One of the themes in Macbeth *is revenge.*

WRITING

adding

Putting more information in your writing to help readers understand it better.

*Adding is one way to **revise** your writing.*

Example:
I love my dog.
Adding:
I love my dog because he is fun to play with.

appropriate form

The kind of writing that is right for its purpose.

*If you want to tell a story, you write **fiction**. If you want to tell someone how to do something, you write **instructions**.*

appropriate word choice

Using words that are right for the subject, the situation, and the **audience**.

*Appropriate word choice is one of the **criteria** of good writing. Choosing the right words helps readers easily understand your writing.*
Compare these sentences in a story for children.

Not appropriate: *The heavy snowfall prevented her from locating the route to the rough shelter.*

Appropriate: *In the deep snow, she lost her way to the cabin.*

WRITING

argue

Writing to give reasons for or against something.

Reading is a very good activity. Books not only help your imagination, they also teach you new words. Plus, you have a lot of fun. That's why everyone should read every day.

audience

The person or persons that the writing is meant for.

*You should choose the **appropriate form** of writing, the language, and the style that are right for your audience.*

"The Three Little Pigs" was written for a children's audience. It has a simple story and simple language.

brainstorming

Writing down everything that comes into your mind about a topic, so you can **organize** the ideas later.

After brainstorming, you can choose the best ideas from your notes and arrange them in order, possibly in an outline.

Brainstorming for writing about music might look like this:

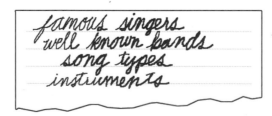

famous singers
well known bands
song types
instruments

WRITING

coherence

The way all the sentences in a paragraph fit smoothly together and support the same **main idea**.

*Coherence is one of the **criteria** of good writing. The sentences and ideas should be arranged and expressed so that the reader can easily understand what you are trying to say.*

combining

Joining ideas or sentences in your writing to help readers understand it better.

*Combining is one way to **revise** your writing.*

Example:
We went outside. It was cold. The wind blew. We had fun making a snowman.

Combining:
It was cold outside, and the wind blew, but we had fun making a snowman.

criteria

Standards or measures by which you judge something.

This essay is better than my last one because its ideas are more organized.

deleting

Taking information out of your writing to help readers understand your writing better.

*Deleting is one way to **revise** your writing.*

Example:

I have to say that the bedroom was chilly and cold.

Deleting:

The bedroom was cold.

describe

Writing to tell what something is like.

I like the apartment we live in. It's small but comfortable. My mother has made it look nice with curtains and pictures. It is high up in the building, and we can see the river from our windows. The neighbors are friendly.

draft

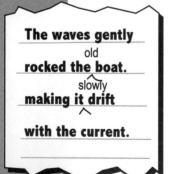

The waves gently
old
rocked the boat.
slowly
making it drift

with the current.

A rough version of what you want to write.

It is helpful to write two or more drafts of your writing, so you can change them until they are in the best form you can make them.

WRITING

editorial

An **essay** that gives the writer's **opinion**, usually in a newspaper.

Here's an example from a local newspaper:

> It is time the government helped the schools. The schools are old and need repair. More and more students are coming each year.

elaborating

Explaining an idea in more **detail** to help readers understand it better.

*Elaborating is one way to **revise** your writing.*

Example:
The window in my bedroom was broken.

Elaborating:
The window in my bedroom was broken, letting in the cold air and making the curtains dance.

entertain

Writing to **entertain** is writing to make readers laugh or keep them interested.

***Tall tales** are examples of writing to entertain.*

WRITING

essay

A short piece of nonfiction writing about a certain topic.

> ### School Life Today
>
> *School life today seems very easy. My parents tell me they had longer school days and more homework when they were in school. But they also say they think we learn more. Maybe this is because we have many more things we can do in school, such as team sports, music, and drama.*

explain

Writing to make something clear.

> ### How I Joined the Swim Team
>
> *I learned to swim because my sister was on the swimming team. However, I only wanted to swim for fun. Then I became good at it. When the swimming coach saw me swim, she said I should join the team. I did, and I really enjoy it.*

express

Writing what you think or feel about certain things.

A diary is an example of writing to express ideas.

WRITING

formal language

The normal words and expressions that anyone can understand.

This book is written in formal language.

influence

To write to change the way people act or think.

I think you should play soccer. Soccer helps you stay healthy. It also makes you feel good about yourself.

inform

To write to give information or knowledge to the reader.

The first people to live in New York City were from Holland. They began the city in 1610 and called it New Amsterdam. Later, the British took over the city and named it after the Duke of York.

informal language

The words and expressions you use with your family and friends.

"Hi, Alana! How's it going?"

WRITING

instructions

Writing to tell the reader how to do something.

To assemble this toy, first lay out all the pieces on a table. Next make sure you have all the pieces shown on the list. Then start with Step One in the directions.

journal

Writing that tells what happens each day.

> **Monday.** Soccer practice was hard. I was very tired afterward.
>
> **Tuesday.** Soccer practice was more fun today. We split the team in two and played against each other.
>
> **Wednesday.** We got our team shirts today in soccer practice. My shirt is big, but I like it anyway. Practice was short today.

learning log

Journal in which you write what you learned.

I learned about negative numbers today. It was hard at first, but then it was easy to understand.

WRITING

letter

Writing to a particular person in a special form.

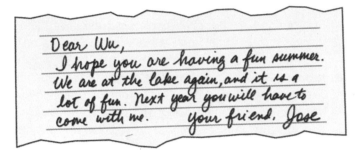

Dear Wu,
I hope you are having a fun summer. We are at the lake again, and it is a lot of fun. Next year you will have to come with me.   Your friend, Jose

log

A daily record of simple **facts** or experiences, such as descriptions of weather, or places you visited on vacation.

Wednesday. Arrived in Washington, D.C. Weather was clear.
Thursday. Visited the Capitol and the Washington Monument.
Friday. Went on tour of the White House.

logical support of ideas

Giving only information that helps the **main idea** of a paragraph or essay.

Logical support of ideas helps give **coherence** _to writing. It means that any_ **detail** _that does not support the_ **main idea** _should be taken out._

Cooking is a lot of fun. ~~My aunt likes to cook.~~ _You can use your own ideas to create foods. You can cook with your friends. You can even have a party to eat what you have cooked._

WRITING

narrate

To tell a story.

> When the stranger came into town, people stared at him. He was old but tall and strong, and his clothes were dirty. Who was he? Where did he come from? No one knew. And no one asked.
>
> Most people were afraid of him. But one little girl was not afraid. One day, the stranger stopped to look at the goods in a store window. The girl came out of the store with her mother. The girl tugged at the man's sleeve. "Hello," she said. "My name is Tina. What's your name?" The man smiled at her and said, "Hello, Tina. My name is Joaquin. I lived in this town once, when I was boy, long ago."

notes

Birthday Party

movies

games

bowling

skating

What you write down when you are **brainstorming** or finding out information.

*Taking notes on what you think, read, see, or hear about a subject helps you remember important ideas to write about. Notes also make it easier to **organize** your ideas.*

organize

To put your ideas in the right order.

Writing about a president's life:

Early childhood
High school and college
First job
How he became president

WRITING

outline

A written list of ideas in the right order.

My Favorite Pet

1. *Introduction*
2. *Pets we have*
       a. Goldfish
       b. Hamster
       c. Dog
3. *Our dog Sami*
       a. Mixed breed
       b. Big, hairy, sloppy
       c. Sleeps next to my bed
4. *Conclusion – Sami is my favorite pet*

---

persuade

To write to get someone to act or think as you want.

We should all work together to clean our parks. Many people have fun at parks. You can see animals and exercise there. By keeping parks clean, more people can enjoy them.

precise wording

The exact or best words for the job in a piece of writing.

You should try to choose the words that best say what you mean when you write.

Example:

Max walked very fast to the school.
Max walked ran to the school.

presentation

A talk about someone or something.

Raul used charts to give a good presentation about how Congress works.

prewriting

The important first stage of preparing your ideas before you write.

*Prewriting includes using **brainstorming, graphic organizers, logs, notes**, and **outlines**.*

problem solve

To write to show how to fix something that is wrong or not going well.

> *Lots of new students come to our school each year. They have come to live in a new town. They don't know the school, and they don't have friends here. Maybe each new student should have someone from the class to help him or her.*

WRITING

progression

The way ideas are arranged in writing so one idea or action leads to another.

A logical progression of ideas helps give **coherence** *to writing.*

If the ideas in this paragraph were arranged differently, it wouldn't make good sense:

> *Francisco's brother Tadeo was having his birthday in just a few days. Francisco wasn't sure what to give him as a present. He thought hard. Tadeo didn't like games, so he wouldn't buy him a game. Tadeo did not listen to music, so he wouldn't buy him a CD. But then Francisco remembered that Tadeo liked reading books about sports. Francisco went to the book store and found just what Tadeo would like – a book about soccer.*

proofread

To check your writing word by word, to make sure there are no mistakes in your writing.

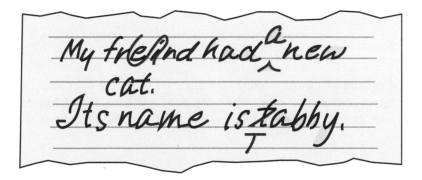

publish

To produce writing for other people to read.

*Personal writing, such as diaries and **journals**, may be written only for yourself. When you write for your friends, your class, or your teacher, you publish your writing.*

rearranging

Putting the ideas in your writing in a different order to make the meaning clearer.

*Rearranging is one way to **revise** your writing.*

Example:
The window in my bedroom was broken, letting the cold air in and making the curtains dance.

Rearranging:
Cold air made the curtains dance as it blew through the broken window in my bedroom.

report

To write to tell a reader what happened.

A picture was broken today. It happened when the door was blown shut by the wind. When the door slammed, the picture fell from the wall. When the picture hit the floor, the glass broke.

WRITING

request

To write to give reasons why you should be allowed to do or have something.

I would like to stay up a half hour later every night. I get all my homework done on time. I'm getting good grades at school. May I get an extra half hour?

review

Gives the good and bad points of a book, television show, or movie.

The first time I saw this show, I liked it a lot. It was funny and interesting. The characters seem just like people I know.

revise

To improve your writing by changing the amount of information in it, or by rearranging or rewriting it.

*When you revise, you write a new **draft**. You revise by **adding**, **deleting**, **combining**, or **rearranging** information, or by **elaborating** or rewriting.*

Math can be fun at times. But you have to ~~try~~ practice a lot.

WRITING

self-monitor

To ask yourself questions to see if you are learning.

When you self-monitor, you are always looking for ways to improve what you do.

Do I know the main idea? What did I learn? Did I check for errors?

transitions

Words or phrases that connect sentences, paragraphs, and ideas in your writing to help readers understand it better.

These are some transitional words and phrases:

For comparing:
but, by comparison, compared to, however, in contrast, meanwhile, on the other hand, yet

For sequence:
after, afterward, before this, finally, first, second, third, next, then

For concluding:
as a result, as I have said, in conclusion, therefore

WRITING

varied sentence structure

A way of making writing interesting by using sentences of different lengths.

*Varied sentence structure is one of the **criteria** of good writing.*

Example:
I was amazed! It was the first time I had won anything in my life. And I had earned it. After so many weeks of hard work, my painting really impressed the judges.

action verb

A word that tells what action someone or something is doing.

jump, runs, ate, sit, play, falls, looked

adjective

A word that describes a **noun** or **pronoun**.

*The **brown** dog lived in a **big** doghouse.*

adverb

A word that describes a **verb**, an **adjective**, or another adverb. Many adverbs end in "-ly."

*Pablo read his book **slowly** because it was **very** good.*

antecedent

The word, **phrase**, or **clause** that is referred to by a **pronoun**.

***Marcos** said **he** would go to the movie.*

***Juanita and Mary** lost **their** keys.*

apostrophe

A **punctuation** mark (') used to show:
(1) that letters have been dropped from a word, or
(2) that something or somebody belongs to another thing or person.

It's raining.

Rosa's pen

*Note that the possessive **its** does not use an apostrophe.*
*The dog found **its** way home.*

capitalization

The use of a capital letter in writing.

*The first word in a **sentence** is capitalized, and **proper nouns** are capitalized.*

*The **R**angers are a baseball team in **T**exas.*

clause

A group of words that has a **subject** and a **predicate**. A **sentence** is made up of at least one clause.

She played piano after school.

***She** is the subject.*
***played piano after school** is the predicate.*

LANGUAGE CONVENTIONS

colon

A **punctuation** mark (:) that is sometimes used to introduce a list.

He had three coins in his pocket: a nickel, a dime, and a penny.

comma

A **punctuation** mark (,) that is used to separate word groups in a **sentence**.

He needs to bring his hat, gloves, and mittens.
For breakfast, we will eat eggs.

common noun

A word that does not name a specific person, place, or thing. Common nouns are not capitalized.

boy, city, fruit, store, water, paper

comparative adjective

A word used to describe the difference between two things.

*Comparative adjectives usually end in **-er**, but longer adjectives use **more**.*

*She is the **taller** of the two sisters.*
*A house is **bigger** than a car.*
*Our team has a **better** chance to win than they do.*
*The roller coaster is **more exciting** than the Ferris wheel.*

LANGUAGE CONVENTIONS

complex sentence

A **sentence** with one **independent clause** and one **dependent clause**.

After she returned from the store, Marta was very tired.

After she returned from the store *is a dependent clause.*
Marta was very tired *is an independent clause.*

compound sentence

A **sentence** with two or more **independent clauses**.

My parents sold our house, and then we went on vacation.

My parents sold our house *is the first independent clause.*
and then we went on vacation *is the second independent clause.*

conjunction

A word that connects two other words or groups of words.

These are some conjunctions:

and	after	since	whenever
but	because	unless	where
for	before	until	wherever
or	if	when	while

*My sister **and** I played in the pool **because** the sun was out.*

contraction

The shortened form of a word with an **apostrophe** to show where a letter or letters are missing. The apostrophe often takes the place of "o" in "not."

*I **can't** go with you until 3:30.*
*Please **don't** forget to meet me then.*

dependent clause

A **clause** that cannot stand alone as a **sentence**.

*She swam **before she went to school**.*

direct object

A **noun** or **pronoun** that receives the action of the **verb**. Direct objects usually answer the questions What? or Whom?

*"Mary brought **cake** to the party."*
*Mary brought what? Answer: **cake***

*"Lily thanked **her**."*
*Lily thanked whom? Answer: **her***

exclamation point

A **punctuation** mark (!) that shows excitement.

I am so happy!
Watch out!

LANGUAGE CONVENTIONS

future tense

The form of a **verb** that shows something is going to happen.

*He **will write** a report for his English teacher.*
*She **will see** monkeys at the zoo.*

helping verb

A **verb** (or verbs) added to another verb that helps to tell more about the time an event happens.

*He **will** write a report for his English teacher.*
*He **has been** writing a report for his English teacher.*

independent clause

A **clause** that can stand alone as a **sentence**.

*After the baseball game, **we went home**.*

indirect object

A **noun** or **pronoun** that shows to or for whom, or to or for what, something is done.

*We gave **Martin** the award.*
*The boys bought their **parents** a gift.*

irregular plural

A **noun** that does not add -*s* or -*es* to make the **plural** form.

Examples:

Singular	Plural
child	children
fish	fish
man	men
mouse	mice
goose	geese

linking verb

A verb (such as *be*, *become*, or *seem*) that connects a **subject** and an **adjective** or **noun**.

Juan **was** first in line.

Carla **is** very nice.

Lok **will be** captain of the soccer team.

Hassan **has become** a good student.

This house **seems** very old.

noun

The name of a person, place, or thing.

Julio brought his **dog** to **America**.

object

The person or thing that receives the action of the **verb**, or follows a **preposition**.

*Tomi closed the **door**. (direct object)*

*The man **in** the **moon** does not really exist. (object of the preposition "in.")*

parts of speech

Kinds of words that name, show an action, describe, or connect other words or groups of words.

The parts of speech are:

noun
pronoun
verb
adjective
adverb
preposition
conjunction

past tense

The form of a **verb** that shows that something happened in the past.

*He **wrote** a report for his English teacher.*

*She **saw** monkeys at the zoo.*

perfect tense

The form of a **verb** that shows a finished action. Usually the **helping verb** "have'" or "has" is used.

*He **has written** a report for his English teacher.*
*She **has seen** monkeys at the zoo.*

period

A **punctuation** mark (.) used at the end of a **sentence**.

Alicia brought her books to class.

phrase

A group of words without a **subject** or **predicate**.

*Annabel was talking **to a friend** who lived next door.*
*Tony was sitting **on a beach**.*

plural

Refers to more than one person or thing. Many plural words end in an **-s**, but not all.

*There were **horses**, **pigs**, and **cows** on the farm.*

possessive

The form of a word used to show that something or somebody belongs to another thing or person.

*Ricardo forgot to bring **his** books.*
*It's **Mom's** turn to choose the game.*

possessive apostrophe

A **punctuation** mark (') used to show that something or somebody belongs to another thing or person.

My sister's shoes are still in her room.

predicate

The part of a **sentence** that says something about the **subject**. The predicate always contains a **verb**.

*Dad **cooked dinner**.*

cooked dinner is the predicate.

***cooked** is a verb, the main part of the predicate.*

preposition

A word that relates a **noun** or **pronoun** to another word in a **sentence**.

Examples:

about	between	in	past
above	by	near	through
at	during	of	under
beside	for	on	until
below	from	over	with

*The dog likes to sleep **under** the stairs.*
*We parked the car **beside** the road.*

LANGUAGE CONVENTIONS

present tense

The form of a **verb** that shows something happening now.

*He **writes** a report for his English teacher.*
*She **sees** monkeys at the zoo.*

progressive tense

The form of a **verb** that shows ongoing action. The verb has "-ing" at the end.

*He is **writing** a report for his English teacher.*
*She is **feeding** the monkeys at the zoo.*

pronoun

A word that takes the place of a **noun**.

*Juanita said **she** was too tired to go to the movie.*
*The girls were sad because **they** wanted her to see it.*

proper noun

The name of a specific person, place, or thing. Proper nouns are **capitalized**.

*The **Alvarez** family went to **Florida** for vacation.*
***Yolanda** walked to **Food World** on **Maple Avenue**.*

LANGUAGE CONVENTIONS

punctuation

Written marks used to give directions to a reader.

question mark

A **punctuation** mark (?) used at the end of a question.

Where are we going?

Did you finish your homework?

semicolon

A **punctuation** mark (;) used to join **independent clauses** with closely connected ideas.

My aunt and uncle have three children; they have one girl and two boys.

sentence

A group of words with a **subject** and a **predicate**, that expresses a complete thought.

I will ride the bus home today.

Subject: *I*
Predicate: *will ride the bus home today*

simple sentence

A sentence made up of one **independent clause**.

My sisters baked bread.

singular

Refers to just one person or thing. It is the opposite of **plural**.

*A **cat** is sitting on the **floor**.*

subject

The person or thing that performs the action of a **sentence**.

***Maria** wanted to buy mangos at the store.*
*The **soccer ball** only just missed the goal.*

subject-verb agreement

A rule stating that when the **subject** of a **sentence** is singular, the **verb** must be singular. Also, when the subject of a sentence is **plural**, the verb must be plural.

***He is sitting** by the window.*
*In this sentence, the subject **He** and verb **is sitting** are both singular.*

***We are sitting** by the window.*
*In this sentence, the subject **we** and verb **are sitting** are both plural.*

LANGUAGE CONVENTIONS

superlative adjective

Used to compare three or more things.

*Superlative adjectives usually end in –est, but longer adjectives sometime use **most**.*

> *He is the **oldest** of three brothers.*
>
> *We have the **greatest** team in the country.*
>
> *She had the **shiniest** shoes in the class.*
>
> *This is the **most beautiful** flower in the garden.*

verb

A word showing an action or state of being.

*Anna **is playing** basketball.*
*Lucy **stayed** home with her sister.*

verb tense

A form of a **verb** that shows the time of an action.

> They **eat** lunch. (present tense)
>
> They **are eating** lunch. (progressive tense)
>
> They **have eaten** breakfast. (perfect tense)
>
> They **will eat** supper. (future tense)

format

The general plan or arrangement of a written work.

*Please organize your paper according to the proper **format**. Show the title and headings, and list your sources at the end.*

primary source

A personal or first-hand account written by someone who lived during a particular time period or event.

The Diary of Anne Frank, *a true story written by an actual victim of the Holocaust, is a primary source.*

public document

A document that deals with people and their government.

Both the Constitution of the United States and population records are public documents.

reference materials

Sources used to provide general information, such as a dictionary, thesaurus, or encyclopedia.

I went to the library to find reference materials for my paper on rivers.

ReSeArcH

research

To find and collect information on a particular subject.

I would like to research causes of war.

secondary source

Sources, such as encyclopedias, textbooks, and magazine articles, that provide information about a historical event but are not a **primary source.** These sources might be published many years after the event happened.

A magazine article about Anne Frank's experience is a secondary source.

source

A place from which you can get information. Sources can be **primary** or **secondary**.

*The teacher asked us to use at least ten **sources** for our research report.*

subject area

A specific topic about which a person studies, discusses, or writes.

The subject area Mr. Mohan really likes to discuss is large birds.

thesis

What your paper is mostly about. In a report, the thesis is the basic argument you are expected to prove.

As the title of my thesis suggests, I will prove that "Students Are Healthy Eaters."

INDEX

M

main idea, 11
make inferences, 11
metaphor, 21
meter, 21
mood, 21
multiple meaning
   word, 2
myth, 21

N

narrate, 36
narrative, 22
nonessential information,
11
nonfiction, 22
notes, 36
novel, 22
noun, 50

O

object, 51
opinion, 11
organize, 36
origin, 3
outline, 37

P

paraphrase, 12
parts of speech, 51
past tense, 51
perfect tense, 52
period, 52
personification, 22
persuade, 37
phrase, 52
playwright, 23
plot, 23
plural, 52
poetry, 23
point of view, 23

possessive, 52
possessive apostrophe, 53
precise wording, 37
predicate, 53
predict, 12
prefix, 3
preposition, 53
presentation, 38
present tense, 54
preview, 12
prewriting, 38
primary source, 58
problem, 12
problem solve, 38
progression, 39
progressive tense, 54
proofread, 39
pronoun, 54
proper noun, 54
public document, 58
publish, 40
punctuation, 55

Q

question mark, 55

R

rearranging, 40
record, 13
reference materials, 58
report, 40
request, 41
research, 59
resolution, 24
review, 41
revise, 41
root, 3

S

scene, 24
secondary source, 59

self-monitor, 42
semicolon, 55
sentence, 55
sequence, 13
setting, 24
short story, 24
simile, 25
simple sentence, 56
singular, 56
solution, 13
source, 59
stage, 25
stanza, 25
style, 25
subject, 56
subject area, 59
subject-verb
   agreement, 56
suffix, 4
summarize, 13
superlative adjective, 57
syllable, 4
symbol, 26
synonym, 5

T

tall tale, 26
theater, 26
theme, 26
thesis, 59
timeline, 14
time order, 14
transitions, 42

V

varied sentence
   structure, 43
Venn diagram, 15
verb, 57
verb tense, 57
vowels, 5